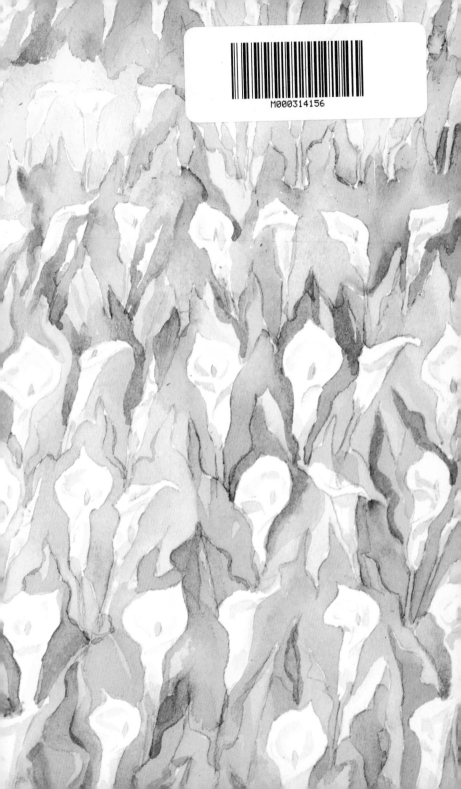

M000314156

# Prayers & Answers

# Prayers & Answers

A Keepsake of God's Handiwork

**Chariot**VICTOR
PUBLISHING
A DIVISION OF COOK COMMUNICATIONS

# THE
## Evelyn Christenson
### COLLECTION

❖ *My First Journal of Prayer*

❖ *Prayerful Thoughts of Encouragement*

❖ *Prayerful Thoughts of Praise*

❖ *Photo Frame*

❖ *Magnets*

Victor Books is an imprint of ChariotVictor Publishing
Cook Communications, Colorado Springs, CO 80918
Cook Communications, Paris, Ontario
Kingsway Communications, Eastbourne, England

Prayers and Answers, A Keepsake of God's Handiwork
© 1997 by Evelyn Christenson

Unless otherwise noted, Scripture quotations are taken from the *Holy Bible, New International Version®*. Copyright © 1973, 1978, 1984 International Bible Society. Used by permission of Zondervan Publishing House.

Scripture quotations followed by "NASB" are taken from the *New American Standard Bible,* © Copyright The Lockman Foundation 1960, 1962, 1963, 1968, 1971, 1972, 1973, 1975, 1977. Used by permission.

Scripture quotations followed by "KJV" are taken from the *Holy Bible, King James Version.*

This book contains adaptations from the following books by Evelyn Christenson: *A Journey into Prayer; Gaining through Losing; What Happens When Gods Answers Prayer; What Happens When We Pray for Our Families; What Happens When Women Pray; Lord, Change Me.*

Editorial contributions by Nancy Parker Brummett
Design by Bradley L. Lind
Illustrations by Barbara Rhodes

First printing, 1997
Printed in Korea.
01 00 99 98 97               5 4 3 2 1

# Table of Contents

# Introduction

I have kept written records of what God said to me in the Bible and the prayers I prayed to Him, since I was 18 years old. As I hid the truths in my heart and applied them to my life, they have produced an incredible walk with Him. Now at 75, God still recalls to my mind, when I need them, these *keepsakes* that He used to lead me, step by step, through joys, successes, difficulties and tragedies.

As the years have gone by, God put these truths together by topics, producing all the books I have written. So, here are a few of the *keepsakes* gleaned from those books—to encourage you in this incredible process.

# How to use this Prayer Journal

As you pray, base your confidence and faith in what the Bible says. Remember, God speaks to you through the reading of His Word. Your prayer is you speaking to God.

In this journal are the *3 steps* I have discovered through the years of seeking to have a deeper and fuller personal relationship with God. I am passing them on in the hope they will not only enrich but explode your prayer life as they have mine.

*Step One:* When you pray, record your prayer and the date under the heading "My Prayer." You will then *recognize* whatever God does in your life on that subject as an answer to that prayer.

Also, when God's answer does not come immediately, your recorded prayer will *remind* you that you prayed about it, and its coming to pass was not just happenstance or luck—but God at work.

Your initial recorded and dated prayer will be the basis of the *keepsake activity* on that subject from then on.

*Step Two:* Record "God's Answer" and date it.
1. If you ask God to change your attitude, watch for how He brings that about in your life.
2. If you make a promise to God about His scriptural truth, know He's smiling at your request and affirming that promise as His will.

3. If you ask for forgiveness, rest on 1 John 1:8-9, that He *has* forgiven you.

4. If you ask God to teach you something, stay alert to all He allows or sends that may be His teaching tools.

5. If you ask for something specific:

   A. When God's answer is "yes," this is your source of praise—a very important step in the prayer process. Date this answer in your journal, and fervently thank and praise Him.

   B. When the answer is "not what you prayed," record what did happen. It is important to record God's "no" answer so you can do Step Three in this journal.

   C. When you do not get an "instant answer," it does not mean God is not at work on it. He knows when to answer—when the thing or person you prayed for is ready, when you are spiritually prepared. God may have intermediate steps to take you through in preparation for His ultimate answer at a future date. Be on the alert for God's answer to that initial prayer—however long it takes.

When your prayers were not answered "the way you hoped," search the Scriptures for possible reasons "why." It could be sin in your life (1 John 3:22), not praying God's will (1 John 5:14-15), praying with the wrong motive (James 4:3), not praying in faith (Hebrews 11:6) or not being able to pray "in the name of Jesus" as your Savior (John 16:14). However, if you *still* don't see a reason, know, with absolute assurance, that God is working out the answer in the best possible way for you and will reveal it to you in His way and His time.

*Step Three:*  Fill in "My Response to God." This is crucial to a meaningful prayer life.

1. Record your *initial response* as soon as you recognize God at work in the request. Possible responses are joy, gratitude, relief, disappointment, anger, or resigned acceptance.

2. Then, as God periodically shows you more and more of what He is accomplishing since the initial answer you recorded, keep track of your responses. Analyzing these will thrill your heart and may startle you with how much you are maturing spiritually.

3. Attempt to see God's perspective through the *whys* of His answers. The way He answers reveals to us His sovereign will, His plans, His reasoning, His perspective of that prayer—and Himself. He is the God who never makes a mistake, does all things for our good, is never too early or too late with His perfect answers—fielding the answers out of His omniscient mind.

The most important part of your prayer process is what happens to you through your responses to God's answers. Your response affects your spiritual condition, relationship with God, and the open doors of ministry to which you will be entrusted. This is what God expects to accomplish with His answer in your life or the one for whom you prayed.

God explains in Jeremiah 33:3 (NASB) that the greatest things come from Him after His initial answer:

*"Call to Me,
and I will answer you,
and I will tell you great and mighty
things, which you do not know."*

This journal is a *keepsake* because God continues to work in your life after the initial prayer and answer—as you *"keep going back"* to it, days and even years later. As you reflect on all the wonderful and mysterious ways God has led you through His answers to your prayers, you'll discover His life-changing power in you, and a growing and deepening walk with Him.

For further information on this process, see *What Happens When God Answers Prayer* by Evelyn Christenson.

Selections from Evelyn Christenson's works are indicated by the following abbreviations:

| | |
|---:|:---|
| "Lord, Change Me!" | LCM |
| A Journey into Prayer | JP |
| Gaining through Losing | GTL |
| What Happens When God Answers Prayer | WGAP |
| What Happens When We Pray for Our Families | WPFF |
| What Happens When Women Pray | WWP |

# Praying in God's Will

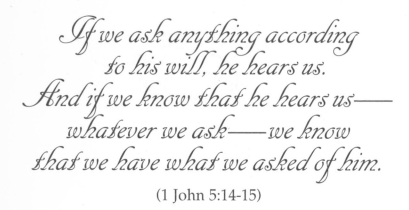

*If we ask anything according to his will, he hears us. And if we know that he hears us— whatever we ask—we know that we have what we asked of him.*

(1 John 5:14-15)

Praying in God's will is not easy, yet it is simple. It involves a complete commitment of our lives to God and His perfect will. This is not a one-time, once-for-all commitment; we have to work at it constantly. It's exciting to live in complete oneness with the will of God. It is never dull or static, but rewarding and fulfilling. (WWP)

## Evelyn's Prayer:

*O God, I want only Your will in my life forever. It is wonderful to live without friction between Your will and my desires. It is awesome to know I can pray what I want, because it is what You want too. Thanks.*

*My Prayer*           *Date*

_____

_____

_____

_____

_____

_____

_____

*God's Answers*       *Date*

_____

_____

_____

_____

_____

_____

_____

*My Response to God*     *Date*

_____

_____

_____

_____

_____

_____

_____

# Meeting the Lord
## in the Morning

---

*In the morning,
O Lord, you hear my voice;
in the morning I lay my requests
before you and wait in expectation.*

(Psalm 5:3)

It's an exciting procedure to wait upon God early in the morning while my mind is fresh, before the "tyranny of the urgent" rushes in or anyone else comes on the scene. Have you learned to say in the morning, "Lord, here I am. Tell me what You want me to know today, what You want me to do." You'll be amazed at His answers! (JP)

---

## Evelyn's Prayer:

*Dear Father, how precious it is for me to meet
You first in the morning so my day will start with Your
presence and direction. I am overwhelmed with joy and
gratitude when I see how You have told me what to write
and how to interact with people and family.*

*My Prayer*                    *Date*

_____
_____
_____
_____
_____
_____
_____

*God's Answers*             *Date*

_____
_____
_____
_____
_____
_____
_____

*My Response to God*       *Date*

_____
_____
_____
_____
_____
_____
_____

# Using God's Word

## For the Word of God is living and active.

(Hebrews 4:12)

There are three steps necessary in using God's Word effectively: (1) accept it, (2) respond to its Author in prayer, and (3) live it. We frequently want to bypass number two and resolutely set our jaws and grit our teeth declaring, "I will not," or stoically set out to obey its commands. But it is only when we interact with God, the Author of these rules and instructions, that we receive the wisdom, grace, strength, power and, most important, the desire to apply them. (JP)

## Evelyn's Prayer:

*Dear Father, forgive me for ever trying to take the Bible as a set of rules instead of talking to You about what You are telling me. Then keep me eager always to do what You have told me.*

*My Prayer*                   *Date*

_____

_____

_____

_____

_____

_____

_____

*God's Answers*            *Date*

_____

_____

_____

_____

_____

_____

_____

*My Response to God*       *Date*

_____

_____

_____

_____

_____

_____

_____

# Plugging into the Power

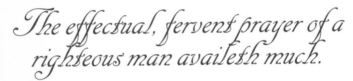

*The effectual, fervent prayer of a righteous man availeth much.*

(James 5:16, KJV)

We work, we pull, we struggle, and we plan until we're exhausted, but we have forgotten to plug into the source of power. And that source of power is prayer—the "effectual, fervent prayer" of a righteous person that is great in its working. How foolish not to plug into the omnipotent power of God. (WWP)

## Evelyn's Prayer:

*Dear God, it seems I have only scratched the surface of the power of prayer. You are the One doing the great and mighty things when I pray. Teach me to plug into Your inexhaustible power more every day.*

*My Prayer*        *Date*

_____

_____

_____

_____

_____

_____

_____


*God's Answers*        *Date*

_____

_____

_____

_____

_____

_____


*My Response to God*        *Date*

_____

_____

_____

_____

_____

_____

# Keeping Sin from Blocking Prayer

---

*If I had cherished sin in my heart, the Lord would not have listened.*

(Psalm 66:18)

Any sin can muddy up our communication with God. When we try to get through to Him in prayer, there may be something in the way—an attitude, a spoken word, or an act. God calls these things sin, and He wants them cleared up. He doesn't want anything between Him and us. If there is, His ears are closed to our prayers, and it's our fault not His. (WWP)

---

## Evelyn's Prayer:

*Dear Father, please bring to my mind the sin or sins that keep You from hearing my prayers. I confess they are sins. Please forgive me. Thank You, Lord, for cleansing me as You promised in 1 John 1:9 and qualifying me for effectual prayer.*

## My Prayer                    Date

_____
_____
_____
_____
_____
_____
_____

## God's Answers                Date

_____
_____
_____
_____
_____
_____
_____

## My Response to God           Date

_____
_____
_____
_____
_____
_____
_____

# God Never Makes a Mistake

---

*O, the depth of the riches of the wisdom and knowledge of God! How unsearchable his judgments, and his paths beyond tracing out!*

(Romans 11:33)

God may answer our prayers not only when we least expect, but He may answer in a way we don't expect. We will be astounded at how God answers prayer. He may answer in a way that is completely opposite to the way we think He should. He knows what is best for us, and He never makes a mistake. (WWP)

---

## Evelyn's Prayer:

*Dear Father, thank You that You know all the "what ifs" in my life. Thank You for caring enough to answer my prayers in the way that is best. I am so grateful and overwhelmed when I see that You never made a mistake in my life.*

*My Prayer*        *Date*

_____

_____

_____

_____

_____

_____

_____

*God's Answers*        *Date*

_____

_____

_____

_____

_____

_____

_____

*My Response to God*        *Date*

_____

_____

_____

_____

_____

_____

_____

# Listening to God

## Be still and know that I am God.

(Psalm 46:10)

Somehow we think we have to talk at God all the time, but there are marvelous things God wants to say to us. He has answers to our questions, secrets He wants to share, and yet we bombard Him with our "much praying." We forget that God is on His throne waiting to say something to us, if we would only give Him a chance.
(WWP)

## Evelyn's Prayer:

*Dear God, thank You for the incredible things You tell me when I stop talking at You. Forgive me for praying as if what I have to say is more important than what You have to say. Help me to be still and listen to the depth of the wisdom You have for me.*

# My Prayer                    Date

_____

_____

_____

_____

_____

_____

_____

# God's Answers                Date

_____

_____

_____

_____

_____

_____

_____

# My Response to God           Date

_____

_____

_____

_____

_____

_____

_____

# Christs Is Among Us

*"For where two or three are gathered*
*together in my name,*
*there am I in the midst of them."*

(Matthew 18:20, KJV)

Whatever we do, we must never underestimate the
value of small group prayer. Christ promised that
where two or three of His followers are gathered
together in His name, He will be in their midst. What
a precious opportunity it provides to practice the
presence of Christ in our small prayer groups. (WWP)

## Evelyn's Prayer:

*Dear Father, thank You for the privilege of Jesus'*
*presence in our prayer groups. Thank You for the joy that*
*this wonderful dimension of Jesus brings us. Keep me*
*faithful to praying with others.*

## My Prayer                Date

_____

_____

_____

_____

_____

_____

_____


## God's Answers            Date

_____

_____

_____

_____

_____

_____

_____


## My Response to God       Date

_____

_____

_____

_____

_____

_____

_____

# Praying in Secret

*"But when you pray, go into your room, close the door and pray to your Father, who is unseen. Then your Father, who sees what is done in secret, will reward you."*

(Matthew 6:6)

Christ recognized the need for spending time alone with God. What a tremendous example Christ's prayer life is to us. Even though He was God Incarnate, He withdrew to a mountain to pray all night before choosing the 12 Apostles. If He thought it necessary, why not us? (WWP)

## Evelyn's Prayer:

*Lord, give me the joy of secret closet praying. Keep me faithful to shut the door and spend time with You and Your Word in secret. Teach me to draw apart, no matter where I am or with whom, to be alone with You.*

*My Prayer*     *Date*

---
---
---
---
---
---
---

*God's Answers*    *Date*

---
---
---
---
---
---
---

*My Response to God*  *Date*

---
---
---
---
---
---
---

# God's Open Doors

*"I know your deeds. See, I have placed before you an open door that no one can shut. I know that you have little strength, yet you have kept my word and have not denied my name."*

(Revelation 3:8)

Has God put before you an open door?
Are you hesitating, perhaps rebelling, or holding back because of fear? God is challenging, "Look, there's an open door, wouldn't you like to walk through it for Me? This is My will for you." (WWP)

## Evelyn's Prayer:

*O God, here I am. I really do want only what You want for me. Open the doors You have for me. Although I know I can't do it alone, I know You will give me the strength and grace to go through them—just as you always have! Thanks, dear Lord.*

*My Prayer*                    *Date*

_____
_____
_____
_____
_____
_____
_____
_____

*God's Answers*                *Date*

_____
_____
_____
_____
_____
_____
_____
_____

*My Response to God*           *Date*

_____
_____
_____
_____
_____
_____
_____
_____

# Drawing Near to Him

Come near to God
and he will come near to you.

(James 4:8)

The joy that floods my whole being as I find myself
visualizing all that God is—His love, His power, His
concern for me—defies description. What greater
privilege could there be for a human being than to
actually come near to the all-powerful, all-knowing God,
high and lifted up on His throne in glory? This is the
most precious part of my prayer time. (WWP)

## Evelyn's Prayer:

*O God, thank You that You have given me the indescribable
experience of drawing into Your awesome presence. Give me
the discipline I need to set aside a special time each day to draw
near to You in prayer.*

*My Prayer*          *Date*

_____
_____
_____
_____
_____
_____

*God's Answers*          *Date*

_____
_____
_____
_____
_____
_____

*My Response to God*          *Date*

_____
_____
_____
_____
_____
_____

# We Come Believing

---

And without faith it is impossible
to please God, because anyone who
comes to him must believe that he exists,
and that he rewards those who
earnestly seek him.

(Hebrews 11:6)

Much happens when we pray. And answers come as we
pray in faith believing. We come believing that God is,
and then believing unequivocally that He rewards those
who seek Him. We do not drop our intercessory prayers
into a bottomless barrel. We send them up to a heavenly
Father who, in His time, in His way, according to His
will, answers them down here on Earth. (WWP)

---

## Evelyn's Prayer:

*Holy God, thank You for showing me that You do answer
my prayers. Increase my faith in You when, humanly,
things seem so impossible.*

*My Prayer*                    *Date*

_____

_____

_____

_____

_____

_____

_____


*God's Answers*                *Date*

_____

_____

_____

_____

_____

_____

_____


*My Response to God*           *Date*

_____

_____

_____

_____

_____

_____

_____

# Taking the Limits off God

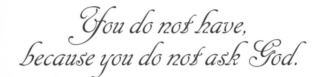

## You do not have, because you do not ask God.

(James 4:2)

God, through His answers, accomplishes what He has wanted to do all along but has been hindered by our lack of prayer. And although He is sovereign and can and does do as He chooses without the help of believers' prayers, He has chosen to operate extensively in this world in response to them. (JP)

## Evelyn's Prayer:

*Holy God, forgive me for the times I substitute doing for praying. I promise You that I will devote an adequate amount of time to You in prayer so that all I do and say will be filled with Your power. Then my prayers will be helping You change things here on Earth.*

## My Prayer       Date

_____
_____
_____
_____
_____
_____
_____

## God's Answers       Date

_____
_____
_____
_____
_____
_____
_____

## My Response to God       Date

_____
_____
_____
_____
_____
_____
_____

# When We're Suffering

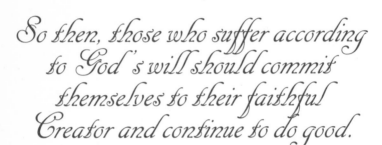

*So then, those who suffer according to God's will should commit themselves to their faithful Creator and continue to do good.*

(1 Peter 4:19)

We, as Christians, aren't promised that we'll be free from suffering. Sometimes we suffer simply because we have frail, human bodies. But if we're committed to the God who doesn't ever make a mistake, we can have the assurance that He has permitted our suffering and has a specific, redemptive reason for it. (JP)

## Evelyn's Prayer:

*Dear Lord, You know how long I have prayed about this physical problem. But You also know how completely I want Your will in my life. Lord, help me to understand that my suffering can be used as a tool to draw me, or others, closer to You.*

*My Prayer*        *Date*

_____
_____
_____
_____
_____
_____
_____

*God's Answers*       *Date*

_____
_____
_____
_____
_____
_____
_____

*My Response to God*      *Date*

_____
_____
_____
_____
_____
_____
_____

# When God Convicts Christians

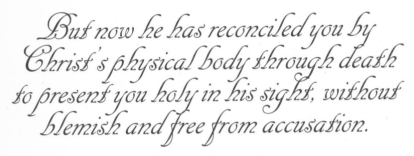

*But now he has reconciled you by Christ's physical body through death to present you holy in his sight, without blemish and free from accusation.*

(Colossians 1:22)

The reason God convicts Christians of sin and demands repentance is so we can be reconciled to Him and, once again, experience beautiful, unbroken  fellowship with Him. It is so that in prayer we can step into that room marked "His holy presence." (JP)

## Evelyn's Prayer:

*O God, I confess that I have violated Your holiness and, thus, our relationship is broken. Please, God, cleanse me from all known and unknown sin. Thank You for being holy enough to be angry at my sin, but loving enough to forgive me and reconcile me to Yourself.*

*My Prayer*         *Date*

_____

_____

_____

_____

_____

_____

_____


*God's Answers*       *Date*

_____

_____

_____

_____

_____

_____

_____


*My Response to God*    *Date*

_____

_____

_____

_____

_____

_____

_____

# An Attitude of Gratitude

*Give thanks in all circumstances,
for this is God's will for you
in Christ Jesus.*

(1 Thessalonians 5:18)

Thanksgiving is a lifestyle. Our ultimate goal is to be
engulfed by, saturated with, and completely controlled
by an attitude of gratitude. Not some emotional high
or an escape from reality, but actually living in a
state of thankfulness—before, during, and
after we receive answers to our prayers. (JP)

## Evelyn's Prayer:

Father, I want to have an attitude of gratitude in all things.
Give me the maturity to trust You enough to be thankful
while I am praying, not just after You give me Your answer.
Although I don't understand this trial in my life right now, I
am thanking You in advance because I trust You completely.

*My Prayer*        *Date*

_____
_____
_____
_____
_____
_____
_____

*God's Answers*       *Date*

_____
_____
_____
_____
_____
_____
_____

*My Response to God*     *Date*

_____
_____
_____
_____
_____
_____
_____

# As the Lord Forgave Us

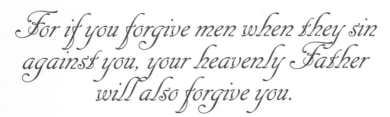

*For if you forgive men when they sin against you, your heavenly Father will also forgive you.*

(Matthew 6:14)

At the end of His earthly life, Jesus prayed to the Father about the requirement of Christians to be reconciled to one another. As long as we are not reconciled to each other, we are sinning because we are disobeying this recorded desire of Jesus. And, of course, as long as there is sin in our lives, we are not reconciled to God. (JP)

## Evelyn's Prayer:

*Lord, help me to forgive that woman who just hurt me. Thank You that, as the members of His body, Jesus insisted on our reconciliation—not so we could become one, but because we are one.*

## My Prayer                    Date

_____
_____
_____
_____
_____
_____
_____

## God's Answers                Date

_____
_____
_____
_____
_____
_____
_____

## My Response to God           Date

_____
_____
_____
_____
_____
_____
_____

# "What Next, Lord?"

⸻ ∞ ⸻

## "Call to me and I will answer you and tell you great and unsearchable things you do not know."

(Jeremiah 33:3)

When God answers a prayer, it is not the final curtain on an episode in our lives. Rather, it is the opening of the next act. The most important part of prayer is what we do with God's answers and how His answers affect us. According to Jeremiah 33:3, there is something after the prayer and after God's answers. Our response to His answers should be, "What next, Lord?" (JP)

⸻ ∞ ⸻

## Evelyn's Prayer:

*Dear Father, help me to look for what You have next for me because of how You answered my prayers. I want to set my mind and heart completely on what You are accomplishing.*

## My Prayer                    Date

_____
_____
_____
_____
_____
_____

## God's Answers                Date

_____
_____
_____
_____
_____
_____

## My Response to God           Date

_____
_____
_____
_____
_____
_____

# Obeying by Not Doing

---

*"For I know the plans I have for you," declares the Lord, "plans to prosper you and not harm you, plans to give you a hope and a future."*

(Jeremiah 29:11)

The hardest part of obedience is being willing not to do something. Obedience isn't only going and doing—but sometimes not going and not doing! It is especially hard when a position or job would bring prestige, honor, and seems so right or necessary. But when we are willing to decrease so that He and His kingdom may increase, this is true obedience. (JP)

---

## Evelyn's Prayer:

*Dearest Lord, forgive me for all the times I have stubbornly gone my own way. I won't go through the door I have been shown right now if it is not Your will. I give it back to You, Lord. You decide.*

*My Prayer*                  *Date*

_____

_____

_____

_____

_____

_____

_____


*God's Answers*            *Date*

_____

_____

_____

_____

_____

_____


*My Response to God*      *Date*

_____

_____

_____

_____

_____

_____

_____

# When We Don't Know How to Pray

*In the same way, the Spirit helps us in our weakness. We do not know what we ought to pray for, but the Spirit himself intercedes for us with groans that words cannot express.*

(Romans 8:26)

There are those times when we don't know how to pray for our families. But God has provided the solution. The Father gave us the Holy Spirit, who prays to Him whatever is the Father's will when we don't know how to pray. (WPFF)

## Evelyn's Prayer:

*Dear God, how often I agonize over what is the right prayer for something or someone. What a relief it is to be able to turn it over to Your Holy Spirit, living inside me, to pray Your will. Thanks, Lord.*

*My Prayer*          *Date*

_____
_____
_____
_____
_____
_____
_____

*God's Answers*        *Date*

_____
_____
_____
_____
_____
_____

*My Response to God*      *Date*

_____
_____
_____
_____
_____
_____

# Crisscrossing Prayers

---

*Now He [Jesus] was telling them a parable to show that at all times they ought to pray and not to lose heart.*

(Luke 18:1, NASB)

When a bride and groom establish a new Christian home, they start to weave the fabric of which their home will be made.  Of all the things they begin to weave into their newly formed family, prayer is the most important. Love, fidelity, mutual respect, support, and serving each other are all vital, but prayers are the threads of the fabric God uses to hold a family together. (WPFF)

---

## Evelyn's Prayer:

*Dear Father, I have watched you weave us into a strong extended family because of our prayers. Keep me faithful and help me encourage even the smallest members of our family that their prayers, when crisscrossed with ours, will keep weaving the fabric of our strong family.*

*My Prayer*          *Date*

_____

_____

_____

_____

_____

_____

_____

*God's Answers*          *Date*

_____

_____

_____

_____

_____

_____

_____

*My Response to God*       *Date*

_____

_____

_____

_____

_____

_____

_____

# Repent and Believe

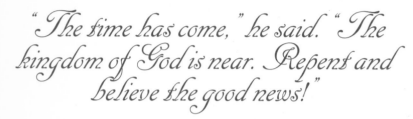

*"The time has come," he said. "The kingdom of God is near. Repent and believe the good news!"*

(Mark 1:15)

Somehow we have reduced becoming a Christian to intellectual acceptance of what even the demons know and believe—Jesus is the Son of God who came to earth, died on the cross, and rose again the third day. But it takes repentance plus belief. Jesus started His preaching with "repent and believe," and the early church was built on repenting and believing in Jesus (Acts 11:18). (WPFF)

## Evelyn's Prayer:

*Dear Lord, thank You that when I was nine, I cried all afternoon about my sins. That evening, they were all forgiven when I asked for Your forgiveness and for Jesus to come into my heart. Help me to faithfully explain this so those listening can make sure their belief isn't just head knowledge.*

## My Prayer                    Date

_____
_____
_____
_____
_____
_____
_____

## God's Answers                 Date

_____
_____
_____
_____
_____
_____
_____

## My Response to God           Date

_____
_____
_____
_____
_____
_____
_____

# Train Up a Child

---

*Train a child in the way he should go,*
*and when he is old*
*he will not turn from it.*

(Proverbs 22:6)

I have been astounded at the lifestyle of some parents
who honestly believed they had brought up their
children "the way they should go." Their gods were
money, career, social status, or pleasure instead of the
godly lifestyle the Bible dictates. Examples in the home of
self-centeredness instead of the biblical caring for others,
amassing treasure on earth instead of heaven, putting the
body above the soul in priorities all directed the children
away from, instead of toward, God. (WPFF)

---

## Evelyn's Prayer:

*O God, examine my heart! Show me all the priorities in my*
*life that are really like the world. Please forgive me. May my*
*every word, hug, and activity bring my precious children and*
*grandchildren closer to You.*

## My Prayer                    Date

_____
_____
_____
_____
_____
_____
_____

## God's Answers                Date

_____
_____
_____
_____
_____
_____
_____

## My Response to God           Date

_____
_____
_____
_____
_____
_____
_____

# Faith Based on Scripture

*All Scripture is God-breathed and is useful for teaching, rebuking, correcting and training in righteousness, so that the man of God may be thoroughly equipped for every good work.*

(2 Timothy 3:16)

It is important to base our faith not on our own whims and wants but on what God says in the Bible. Faith is not blind faith in what we want. It is faith in what God says to us in His Word, the Bible. It is God's doctrine, reproof, correction, and instruction in righteousness that form the basis of what we pray in faith. (WPFF)

## Evelyn's Prayer:

*Dearest Father, forgive me for putting my faith in my own ideas. Keep me believing and obeying Your doctrine and instructions in righteousness, even Your reproof and correction.*

*My Prayer*            *Date*

_____

_____

_____

_____

_____

_____

_____

*God's Answers*         *Date*

_____

_____

_____

_____

_____

_____

_____

*My Response to God*     *Date*

_____

_____

_____

_____

_____

_____

_____

# Faith in What—or Whom?

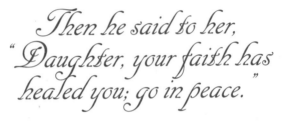

Then he said to her,
"Daughter, your faith has
healed you; go in peace."

(Luke 8:48)

In what or whom do we put our faith when praying?
Faith in our ability to have faith? Faith in the words
printed on a page of the Bible? No. The faith must be in
the God who gave the Bible's promises. (WPFF)

## Evelyn's Prayer:

*Lord, give me the faith of the woman who reached out to touch
the hem of Your garment. May I always seek You, and You
only, as desperately as she did.*

*My Prayer*          *Date*

_____
_____
_____
_____
_____
_____
_____

*God's Answers*          *Date*

_____
_____
_____
_____
_____
_____
_____

*My Response to God*       *Date*

_____
_____
_____
_____
_____
_____
_____

# Forgiving Family Members

---

*Bear with each other and forgive whatever grievances you may have against one another. Forgive as the Lord forgave you.*

(Colossians 3:13)

The most important prayer in the family healing process is one that leads to our being able to forgive loved ones—not just in word, but in our hearts. Forgiving does not mean that we condone what people have done. It does not absolve the sinner of accountability to God or responsibility to the one hurt. Forgiving is the step God provides the victim, to heal his hurt, mend the relationship, and restore the God-intended unity in family relationships. (WPFF)

---

## Evelyn's Prayer:

*Dearest God, when there are bitter words, icy withdrawals, or accusations by family members, it is so easy to retaliate verbally or have bitterness in my heart. O Lord, help me restore our oneness by always forgiving immediately.*

## My Prayer                    Date

_____

_____

_____

_____

_____

_____

_____

## God's Answers                Date

_____

_____

_____

_____

_____

_____

_____

## My Response to God           Date

_____

_____

_____

_____

_____

_____

_____

# Facing Problems as Adults

When I was a child, I talked like
a child, I thought like a child,
I reasoned like a child.
When I became a man,
I put childish ways behind me.

(1 Corinthians 13:11)

God deals with us and expects us to deal with hurts as
adults. He certainly is not against our identifying past
abuses. But never dealing with them as grown-ups is less
than God has provided. We must come to a place of being
accountable to Him and responsible to others for our
attitudes. When we're grown, how we handle the hurts
is up to us, and how we handle them determines our
ultimate healing. (WPFF)

## Evelyn's Prayer:

*Dear God, forgive me for ever thinking I had the right to harbor
past hurts like a spoiled child. When I'm the victim, help me to
"break the victim chain" by forgiving.*

## My Prayer                    Date

_____

_____

_____

_____

_____

_____

_____


## God's Answers                Date

_____

_____

_____

_____

_____

_____


## My Response to God           Date

_____

_____

_____

_____

_____

_____

# When God Delays His Answers

---

*My soul finds rest in God alone; my salvation comes from him. He alone is my rock and my salvation; he is my fortress, I will never be shaken.*

(Psalm 62:1-2)

God delays His answers to our prayers for many reasons, even while we are doing what's right. God is in the business of shaping His children. He knows when and how to answer our prayers to make us into what He wants us to be. Cutting short that process by answering our prayers too soon or the way we think He should deprives us of His divine perfecting. (WPFF)

---

## Evelyn's Prayer:

*Lord, thank You for Your perfect timing in answering my prayers. How awesome it has been to see what You were doing during the waiting process. Teach me to trust You completely while I wait.*

*My Prayer*              *Date*

_____

_____

_____

_____

_____

_____

_____


*God's Answers*        *Date*

_____

_____

_____

_____

_____

_____

_____


*My Response to God*     *Date*

_____

_____

_____

_____

_____

_____

_____

# Golden Bowls of Prayer

*And when he had taken it, the four living creatures and the twenty-four elders fell down before the Lamb. Each one had a harp and they were holding golden bowls full of incense, which are the prayers of the saints.*

(Revelation 5:8)

How wonderful to know that after everything that happens to us through God's answers to our prayers, there is one more thing. God feels that our prayers are important enough to preserve and precious enough to enhance in golden bowls before His throne. (WGAP)

## Evelyn's Prayer:

*O Lord, how wonderful to know that my prayers are so precious to You that You save every one of them in golden bowls. Keep me mindful of how important they are to You so I will faithfully keep them coming.*

*My Prayer*         *Date*

_____
_____
_____
_____
_____
_____
_____

*God's Answers*         *Date*

_____
_____
_____
_____
_____
_____
_____

*My Response to God*         *Date*

_____
_____
_____
_____
_____
_____
_____

# For Whose Glory?

---⁂---

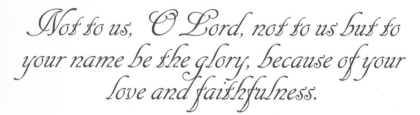

*Not to us, O Lord, not to us but to your name be the glory, because of your love and faithfulness.*

(Psalm 115:1)

Wanting something for our glory, not God's, is one reason why a prayer that may be scripturally accurate and acceptable, is ruined by our motive. We can even have the wrong reason for our prayers to win others to Christ. For whose glory do we want to bear spiritual fruit? Are we trying to win another to Jesus to get credit ourselves? For whose glory? (WGAP)

---⁂---

## Evelyn's Prayer:

*Dear Father, I give to You all the glory for every single thing You do through me. I know it is You working in me, so You alone deserve the glory.*

*My Prayer*            *Date*

_____
_____
_____
_____
_____
_____
_____

*God's Answers*          *Date*

_____
_____
_____
_____
_____
_____
_____

*My Response to God*     *Date*

_____
_____
_____
_____
_____
_____
_____

# Making Restitution

But Zacchaeus stood up and said to the Lord, "Look, Lord! Here and now I give half of my possessions to the poor, and if I have cheated anybody out of anything, I will pay back four times the amount."

(Luke 19:8)

There is no way we can repay God when we violate His holiness. We must repent because we have hurt Him, and do everything in our power to restore our relationship with Him. Then we serve Him with a new passion, making up for the lost days or opportunities. Human relationships are different. Reconciliation to people we have sinned against usually includes making restitution.

## Evelyn's Prayer:

*O God, forgive me for being insensitive. Forgive my selfishness. Father, bring to my mind all those to whom I need to make restitution—and give me Jesus' love for them and the courage to obey You.*

## My Prayer                     Date

_____

_____

_____

_____

_____

_____

_____


## God's Answers                 Date

_____

_____

_____

_____

_____

_____

_____


## My Response to God            Date

_____

_____

_____

_____

_____

_____

_____

# Praying the Wrong Prayer

*When you ask, you do not receive, because you ask with wrong motives, that you may spend what you get on your pleasures.*

(James 4:3)

How can we be sure we are not praying the wrong prayer? First, we must stay in the Bible to become aware of what is right and wrong in God's eyes. This will enable us to identify those prayer requests that are self-motivated. Next, after praying a request, we should wait in God's presence, letting Him examine our reasons for the prayer. (WGAP)

## Evelyn's Prayer:

*Dear Father, show me the wrong prayers I have been praying. Please forgive me when I don't read the Bible enough to know the things for which I ought to pray.*

## My Prayer                    Date

_____

_____

_____

_____

_____

_____

_____

## God's Answers                Date

_____

_____

_____

_____

_____

_____

_____

## My Response to God           Date

_____

_____

_____

_____

_____

_____

_____

# When We're Not Well

Therefore, I urge you, brothers,
in view of God's mercy, to offer your
bodies as living sacrifices,
holy and pleasing to God—this is
your spiritual act of worship.

(Romans 12:1)

God changed me from an overprotective guardian of my body to one who entrusts that body to Him. What a great way to live—no worry, no hassle! Whenever I don't feel well, I say, "Lord, if You want me to be well enough to do the job that's coming up, thank You. But if not, just teach me what You have for me to learn while I'm on a shelf."

(LCM)

## Evelyn's Prayer:

*Dear Father, thank You that You taught me to give
You my body. Thank You for taking away all my anxieties
about my health. This body is Yours, to use for
Your purpose and Your glory.*

*My Prayer*           *Date*

_____

_____

_____

_____

_____

_____

_____

*God's Answers*          *Date*

_____

_____

_____

_____

_____

_____

*My Response to God*      *Date*

_____

_____

_____

_____

_____

_____

# Change Me First

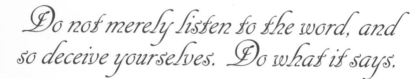

*Do not merely listen to the word, and so deceive yourselves. Do what it says.*

(James 1:22)

I cannot expect those I teach to be changed by applying God's Word if I have not been changed by it first. But that is exactly what happens when I study His Word. The observations are thrilling, the studying is exhilarating, but the change comes when I apply what the Scripture means to my everyday life. (LCM)

## Evelyn's Prayer:

*Lord, I want to be more than a learner of the Bible.*
*Forgive me when its precepts have only been head knowledge.*
*Help me to do everything You teach me.*

## My Prayer                                    Date

_____
_____
_____
_____
_____
_____

## God's Answers                                Date

_____
_____
_____
_____
_____
_____

## My Response to God                           Date

_____
_____
_____
_____
_____
_____

# God's Standard

*Jesus Christ is the same yesterday and today and forever.*

(Hebrews 13:8)

God's standard doesn't change—His yardstick of perfection is not shortened by years or culture, His purpose to conform me to the image of Christ is the same yesterday, today, and forever. When I know what God's instructions meant to its initial recipients, I can apply the same truths to my life today. (LCM)

*Evelyn's Prayer:*

*Lord, I know I am to be blameless and acceptable in Your sight. Your moral law does not change. Please keep me sensitive to what You call right and wrong in Your holy Word and to always living accordingly.*

## My Prayer                    Date

_____
_____
_____
_____
_____
_____
_____

## God's Answers                Date

_____
_____
_____
_____
_____
_____

## My Response to God           Date

_____
_____
_____
_____
_____
_____

# "Why, Lord?"

## "My ears had heard of you, but now my eyes have seen you."

(Job 42:5)

During the early years of marriage, I found myself almost drowning in a sea of "why" questions as trials flooded over me—and I knew I could not bear them. Gradually, I detected a pattern. It was in those times of engulfment in a sea of sorrows—lost babies, wars, surgeries, and calamities—that God spoke to me in a new way. As with Job in his sorrows, God chose to reveal Himself to me at those times, showing me a deeper, more profound side of Himself—one I'd never seen before. (GTL)

## Evelyn's Prayer:

*O God, I hear so much of You, but thanks for showing me Your real self in my sorrows. Please keep turning my "whys" into my "who"—You, my God!*

My Prayer                    Date

_____

_____

_____

_____

_____

_____

_____


God's Answers                Date

_____

_____

_____

_____

_____

_____

_____


My Response to God           Date

_____

_____

_____

_____

_____

_____

_____

# The Secret Is in the Losing

*For whoever wants to save his life will lose it, but whoever loses his life for me will find it. What good will it be for a man if he gains the whole world, yet forfeits his soul?*

(Matthew 16: 25-26)

We frantically scurry around looking for life in the things we have and do, when all along the secret is in the losing. We can't be filled with two things at one time, so it is a matter of being emptied—emptied so that Christ can fill us with Himself. I have discovered the secret of finding radiant, abundant life—losing life for Jesus' sake. (GTL)

## Evelyn's Prayer:

*O God, it seems backward to lose something in order to gain it. But how true it has been in my life. Help me to keep losing my life until there is nothing left but Christ!*

## My Prayer                    Date

_____

_____

_____

_____

_____

_____

_____


## God's Answers                Date

_____

_____

_____

_____

_____

_____


## My Response to God           Date

_____

_____

_____

_____

_____

_____

_____

# Strength in Weakness

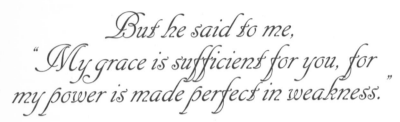

*But he said to me,*
*"My grace is sufficient for you, for*
*my power is made perfect in weakness."*

(2 Corinthians 12:9)

It is not physical strength that counts, but the power of Christ that takes up its abode and pitches its tent over our bodies when we're weak. What was Paul's (or my) maximum strength compared with Christ's omnipotence? In comparison to Christ's infinite, limitless power, all the strength we could ever muster, rolled into one gigantic push, would pale like a firefly competing with a nuclear explosion. (GTL)

## Evelyn's Prayer:

*Holy Father, to feel Your all-sufficient strength filling me when*
*I have been too sick to speak is more than I can comprehend.*
*But I stand in grateful awe and humble gratitude to You.*

*My Prayer*          *Date*

_____
_____
_____
_____
_____
_____
_____

*God's Answers*          *Date*

_____
_____
_____
_____
_____
_____
_____

*My Response to God*      *Date*

_____
_____
_____
_____
_____
_____
_____

# God Comes in Proportion to Our Need

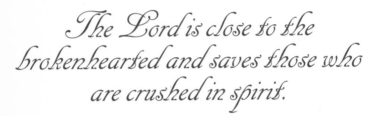

*The Lord is close to the brokenhearted and saves those who are crushed in spirit.*

(Psalm 34:18)

Theologians tell us that God has the ability to be everywhere at once. But does this mean He is in all places at all times in the same proportion? It does not appear so. An amazing characteristic of God's nature, which I have observed, is that He comes in proportion to our needs. The deeper the sorrow, the more comfort He gives; the larger the void, the more God fills it; the greater the need, the more we have of Him. (GTL)

## Evelyn's Prayer:

*O Father, my heart is overwhelmed with gratitude at all the times You have put Your loving arms around me when I couldn't go on. I trust You for every future trial that is sure to come my way.*

# My Prayer                    Date

_____
_____
_____
_____
_____
_____
_____

# God's Answers                Date

_____
_____
_____
_____
_____
_____
_____

# My Response to God           Date

_____
_____
_____
_____
_____
_____
_____

# Reaching Our Children

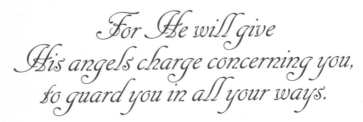

*For He will give
His angels charge concerning you,
to guard you in all your ways.*

(Psalm 91:11, NASB)

How can a simple thing like prayer do such a
monumental job in our families? When our children
have rebelled and broken the family ties, prayer calls on
God who always can and will reach down to them no
matter where they are scattered around the earth.
He will intervene in their lives no matter what they are
doing. This is the God who can muster ten thousand
angels to protect them in the most dangerous situations
and rescue them in all crises—if we pray. (WPFF)

## Evelyn's Prayer:

*O Father, thank You that Your ways are so much
higher than mine. You know and see the big picture for my
family. Help me trust in You and not in my efforts.*

# My Prayer                    Date

_____
_____
_____
_____
_____
_____
_____

# God's Answers                Date

_____
_____
_____
_____
_____
_____
_____

# My Response to God           Date

_____
_____
_____
_____
_____
_____
_____

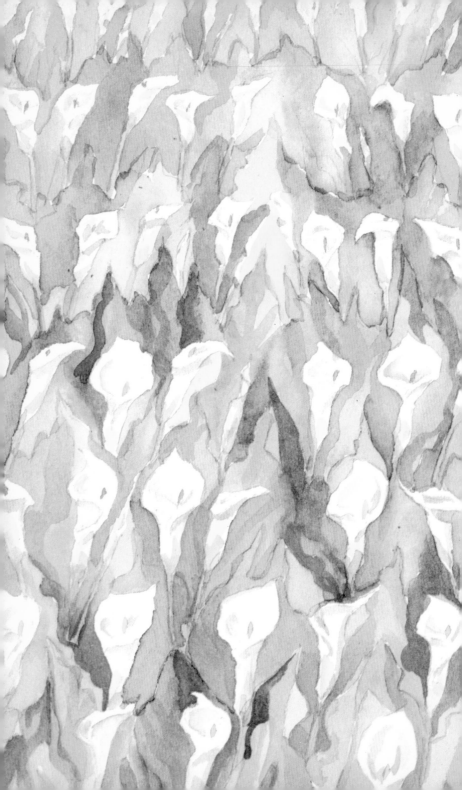